To anyone who has ever dreamed,
dream bigger.

5 RULES FOR NETWORKING WITH MILLIONAIRES & BILLIONAIRES

GERMAINE MOODY

become endless
INTERNATIONAL

ISBN 978-0-578-91412-1

Books may be purchased for education, business, or sales promotional use. For book/author inquiries, including bulk orders, contact BecomeEndlessPublishing@gmail.com.

CONTENTS

Introduction

You don't have to admit it but to some degree we're all either fascinated or disgusted by the life of millionaires and billionaires. Be it disdain or admiration, love or hate, whether you know one personally or not, you've probably already formed an opinion. I like to call them "Millies" and "Billies" for short, so for the duration of this writing, we'll roll with those terms. Who wouldn't want a millie or billie as a friend, colleague, confidant, business partner? Truthfully, I think everyone does but for most that would just be wishful thinking. Thanks to networking, technology and the five rules listed in this book, your wishful thinking can now become reality.

Social networking, defined as "the use of dedicated websites and applications to interact with other users, or to find people with similar interests to oneself", has changed everything, even though humans have been networking for all of history. This wave of technology ushered in an unprecedented and global saturation of online networking social networks, networking groups, networking companies, networking events, and a worldwide networking movement. It has connected almost everyone on planet Earth, making most humans one click away from networking with anyone anywhere in the world. Millies and Billies are no exception, matter of fact, they are some of the most connected and networking people that exist. If you want to connect with them, get in their circles or eventually become one yourself, I've discovered that it's not as far-fetched as you may have imagined. It's just a matter of learning, activating, then mastering the rules of the game.

1

Become A Leader And Lead

The first thing you must do is to become a leader, plain and simple. Leadership is a magnet to the rich and powerful. They are attracted to leaders, people that stand up, stand out, get things done and make things happen. It doesn't matter what you're leading, though hopefully not some destructive cult, but it does matter that you become a leader and actually lead. This can be in a variety of areas such as your community, philanthropy, the arts, academia, business, agriculture, medicine, religion and so on. If you interview five hundred self-made millies and billies, you'll discover that you have five hundred leaders in front of you. Like-minded people operate in the same circles. If you want in, you'll need to wake up and draw out the leader within you.

We spend most of our lives, especially the early years, being led by others. So as we get older, we tend to stick to the flow of following the leader instead of becoming one ourselves. This could also help explain why only 1% of the population has more wealth than half of the world. Some of you think you weren't born to be a leader, furthermore you believe many things just aren't meant for you. Well that's just a bunch of bull you've been sold or have been selling to yourself, and you need to stop buying it today. You think this way because it was never brought up in your childhood. The things we learn, experience and remember as children and teenagers often manifest in adulthood, good and bad. A lot of us never heard the words "be a leader", "you can become a millionaire" or "you can become a billionaire" in our home growing up. So the idea of becoming any of those is close to nonexistent in our minds.

Becoming a leader may cause you to be the first in your family to believe, do, pursue or achieve it. We see this all the time; a son being the first to graduate college, a daughter becoming the first doctor in the family, a dad being the first to run for public office and win, someone becoming the first this or that, it happens often but not enough. Leadership comes with a lot of firsts, and if you want in with those who like being first the majority if not all the time, then this is your official notice that it's time to lead. Don't worry, I'll share ways to discover what you're supposed to lead and ways that you can be a leader. In the meantime, networking requires you to become a leader. Taking charge of your life requires you to become a leader. Building a business requires you to become a leader. Helping others requires you to become a leader. The only way you'll be successful utilizing the rules in this book is by first understanding that you must become a leader and that you are now, at this moment, a leader.

CREATED EQUAL BUT NOT VIEWED EQUAL

At human conception, we're all formed by God as equal. What happens between birth and your adult life defines how you are viewed by the world. Some soar high and some fall swiftly to the ground. Some lead millions of people while others follow every blow of the wind. You don't need special powers to see that society views certain individuals differently than others. This is more than apparent for leaders, including millies and billies. Leaders are held to a higher standard than everyone else. Leaders are also expected to be bold, courageous and positive role models. There are great pressures, requirements, responsibilities, lessons and sacrifices along the journey of and that arrive with leadership, so please understand it's no walk in the park to get there. This is oftentimes a reason why many have a hard time gaining access to certain circles of people. Though networking is designed to be used as a fast track into these circles, the prerequisite still remains, you must become a leader or, your chances of being ignored are greatly magnified. In life there are only two types of people, those that lead and those that follow, or in other words, those that do and those that watch them do it. As a leader you are mandated to seek more, learn more and do more to become more. The world is going to label you as ordinary or extraordinary, there is no inbetween. You want extraordinary because that's where you belong. There's nothing wrong with ordinary but you wouldn't be reading this if you desired anymore ordinary in your life. For most millies and billies, ordinary was never an option, so don't let it be one for you.

LEAD WITH WHAT YOU LOVE AND BECOME GREAT AT IT

We've all heard that you should do what you're passionate about in life. I agree with that but this doesn't mean that every passion should be turned into a career. My advice is to lead with what you love and become great at it. You can be passionate about many things and not good at any of them. I know a lot of passionate people but that's all they have, no talent for the passion, no skill for the passion, no discipline for the passion, no knowledge for the passion, no networking for the passion, which leaves nothing but passion. It's best to focus on those things that you love to do, want to do, have the skills and effort to do which can then be mastered and magnified to make an impact in whatever industry, profession or mission you desire. Sit down, think, and seriously ask yourself, "What would make me miserable for the rest of my life if I don't get a chance to become, add to or change in the world?" Your answers are the desires of your heart and somewhere in there is a clue, the thing or at least a starting point to what you're born to lead at. The true desires of your heart also come with divine assistance to achieve them but you still have to discover them first. It's important not to let passion only be your decision maker because some passions can diminish in desire over time or even change throughout life.

There are natural gifts, skills, talents, passions and interests we're all born with that will lead us to what we love. Your top goal in life should be to search and discover this with great curiosity and soul observation then build up the leader within you so you can start making your life contributions to the world. Some figure it out early as a child or in their teenage years while others do so in their 40's and beyond. On the other hand, you can also lead in things that you don't love and in things that you have no passion for whatsoever. Many do this daily, some become very wealthy, even famous for it. You must decide now how you want to spend the years of your life, whether loving them or loathing them, it's up to you. It may take years or decades to get there but leading with what you love is worth the journey of finding it. Your spirit comes alive, your productivity is maximized and your magnetism becomes undeniable when you're operating and living in the designated position you believe you were created for. The world recognizes it, also millies and billies are drawn to it from thousands and thousands of miles away.

4 WAYS TO LEAD

There are multiple ways you can become a leader. There are different types as well as different levels of leadership. We'll focus on four types that help attract millies and billies the fastest when networking. Many of these leaders help move the world and the human race forward in some way or another, others have simply become masters of their domains.

1. **INVENT.** The first way to become a leader is to invent something that a group of people or the world needs. Inventors create new things and turn ideas into reality. The pros to this is that anyone can be an inventor. The cons to this is that most people ignore their own ideas and creative instincts. It doesn't matter who you are,

where you're from or who you know. It's just a matter of opening your mind, your eyes and your ears, observing daily life through our internal lens for the future. Inventors pay attention to the way things are and how they can be done better, safer, easier or faster. They are the lifeblood of human progression and enable us to take our present and future generation to the next level. If you look around you, everything you see was invented by someone else. If it's a significant invention, then whoever invented it probably became a millie or billie themselves. Entrepreneur millies and billies love being involved with or being the first at bringing new and great inventions to the masses. By becoming an inventor you'll stand out, a lot, matter of fact, you'll become a leader in a league of your own. And there's nothing more attractive to millies and billies when networking than connecting with someone who has carved out their own space in the world, like many of them have.

2. **INNOVATE.** The second way to lead is to become an innovator or what some call a 'game changer'. Inventors and innovators are related, matter of fact a lot of innovators are inventors as

well. Though not always the same, innovators and inventors are still kindred spirits. They are known for taking what was, what is, and then turning it into what could be, what should be and what will be so that it advances, expands or elevates the world. They are game changers, changing the way things were and showing the world how things will be from now on. You can find innovators everywhere, in every profession. People are always discovering new ways, new thoughts and new ideas for past inventions and concepts. Doctors, astronomers, entertainers, teachers, architects, designers, scientists, entrepreneurs, students, everyone can innovate. There's an innovator in all of us, and when it's revealed, millies and billies are drawn to you because iron sharpens iron, and because they are some of the most successful innovators around.

3. **DOMINATE.** The third way to lead is to dominate. This word is used mostly in business, sports, leadership positions and areas where there's lots of competition. Companies, entrepreneurs, athletes, entertainers and anyone who leads in their respective industries, sectors, regions and countries are considered dominators.

Being a dominator requires that you have a strong backbone because as the leader you're constantly placed in the court of public opinion. One that is loved by many and unfortunately despised as well. A lot of millies and billies are familiar with this position all too well so this creates common ground for understanding and for you to network. If you can dominate in your space, be the leader, be voted the best, set the greatest record, be #1 in the world or your region, have the most sale, or these days have the most followers, whatever the case, dominate and you'll have more leverage into prime millie and billie circles. Several of them got to where they are by not competing but instead, by dominating. Being the best, if not one of the best at what you do is a strategy you should definitely use if you can.

4. **EMPOWER.** The fourth way to lead is to empower others, to inspire, motivate and encourage the human spirit. The greatest form of branding is hope. Those who give people hope to continue, assuring them a better day is near or that they too can be successful or amazing are the most sought after leaders in the world. From

spiritual leaders, motivational speakers, entertainers, teachers, entrepreneurs, community leaders, mentors, authors, even some politicians, are what I call the empowerers. Some have built billion dollar global brands around empowerment. Many of the biggest companies and brands use empowerment in some way or another in their marketing and advertising to sell products and services, showing how their brands will bring you joy and happiness, make you feel a part of the 'in crowd' or help you achieve what you want in life. Empowerers can also generate very large followings and become massive forces to be reckoned with. As a solo empowerer of other people, millies and billies are drawn to you and eager to network with you not because of the money you can generate but because of your message of motivation, which they too may have and share as empowers as well. They understand the importance and mandate of positivity and self-motivation in our current world, continuously surrounding themselves with other great empowerers, whether it's family, friends, business colleagues, books, videos, etc.

OUTWORKING OTHERS

They say 'The early bird catches the worm", and what that simply means is that whoever outworks the other has a better chance of success. Over the past ten years of producing and hosting networking events around the world, I've learned that outworking others has played a key role in my success and the access I now have to almost anyone on the planet. Was it difficult to outwork others? Yes. Did I sacrifice almost everything? Yes. Has it paid off? Most definitely. If everyone is doing the same thing, with the same quality, using the same techniques, resources and tools, the only differentiator will be the amount of time you put in to get ahead of others. This goes for life and whatever you pursue. Chances are, someone, somewhere in the world, is planning more than you, strategizing more than you, researching more than you, networking more than you. So in order for you to stay in the game and relevant, you must outwork them. I doubt you'll meet many self-made millionaires or billionaires who'll tell you otherwise. Most of them consistently outworked those around them. It's almost impossible to get to the top if you don't.

Having an incredible work ethic helps attract the world's most successful and wealthiest people to you. Millies and billies know what it takes and finds it refreshing to build relationships with the same. I've seen and experienced the impoverishing effects of laziness. It has become one of the biggest deceptions of the human mind. Truth be told, if you do nothing, you will receive nothing in return. Outworking others is no easy task but it's crucial to your networking success. It's a muscle, that if used on a regular basis, becomes a habit and can expedite you to the greatest heights in life. You'll find yourself doing things that your friends and family members aren't doing, and achieving things they themselves have always dreamed of.

KEY POINTS ✓

- Leadership is a magnet to the rich and powerful.
- For most millies and billies, ordinary was never an option, so don't let it be an option for you.
- Your spirit comes alive, your productivity is maximized and your magnetism becomes undeniable when you're operating and living in the designated position you believe you were created for.
- 4 Ways To Lead: Invent, Innovate, Dominate and Empower.

- If everyone is doing the same thing, with the same quality, using the same techniques, resources and tools, the only differentiator will be the amount of time you put in to get ahead of others.

2

Enhance Who You Are Then Magnify Your Visibility With Crafted Perception

You are not your best yet and will never be your very best because we were created unlimited. The only way to discover your best is to live forever. In the meantime, each day, each month and each year should be dedicated to enhancing who you are, becoming a better you for usage, and then present yourself strategically to the world to attract, build and accomplish whatever you desire using thought-out crafted perception. Many in the public eye have mastered this, so have several millies and billies. Ultimately, you define your own limits and have the power to influence, not control, what others perceive about you.

DON'T JUST BE YOUR   BE YOUR GREATEST SELF

We've all heard people say   said "Just be yourself" to someone, and i   ke those words have been made into law. But the   is, just being yourself won't automaticall   you successful, nor will it guarantee that people   e you, nor will it assure you access to conne   nillies and billies.

Being yourself is only 50% of the equation in life, besides, who else can you be? Only when you become your greatest self through constant personal development, inside and out, will you set yourself in a position to soar above the status quo and the majority who have settled for a much lower state of living. All of the millies and billies I know live by personal development. They are forever expanding their minds, enhancing their physical health, evolving their communication skills, increasing their own value internally and externally to bring more value to their lives and to share with the world.

Think of all the things you know you could do to become a greater person and greater at what you do or desire to do. I have lists and lists of things for myself that I work on. If you've had lots of past business and personal relationships go sour, it may not be their fault, there could be something you need to work on as well. Maybe you need to give yourself more days to make decisions instead of hastily deciding. Could it be that your approach to certain opportunities or people is uncomfortable to some or you may have a bad attitude? Could it be the way you respond to people or how you perceive certain situations? It's tough to analyze yourself and be truthful about your own faults, uncertainties and inconsistencies but you have to or you'll never grow. The key to it all is self-awareness. You become your greatest by ongoing self-examination and remaining in a continual state of awareness. Millies and billies are known to surround themselves with the smartest, greatest, most talented, most curious, most advanced and most unlimited people. They are attracted to those who are mastering and maximizing their own existence. Remove your limits, seek to become greater in all things, and greater in understanding about yourself and others. This opens the door to the unlimited, where opportunities, ideas and people come looking for you.

YOUR THINKING MUST CHANGE TO ESCAPE MEDIOCRITY

"For as he thinketh in his heart, so is he", Proverbs 23:7, one of the most profound and popular scriptures in the Holy Bible and one that I've found to stand true throughout history. The way you think and what you think about yourself is your life source. Your thinking will either elevate you or cause you to self-destruct in due time. If you think you are poor, you will attract things and people that assist you in being poor, and you will pursue and allow things in your life that encourage poverty. If you think you are rich, you will attract things and people that assist you in being rich, and you will pursue and allow things in your life that encourage becoming rich. My thinking leads me to networking with millies and billies, and to becoming one. I always thought and knew I belonged in that same circle. My thinking also led me to write books because I always thought and knew I belonged in that circle. And the list goes on and on in my life.

One of the best ways to change your thinking is to study the way others think that you admire or that you want to emulate. People who inspire us are usually positive minded and they influence our outlook on life. Since we're all composites of one another and more connected than we know, it's wise to take advantage of listening to a variety of positive thinkers, especially leaders. I tell people often that you have to forget everything you've learned that doesn't line up with where your greatest thoughts are, then start your learning process over. Most people aren't raised as kids to think that they can accomplish what is considered impossible. They are raised to follow the rules, instructions, and the scheduling of other people for the rest of their lives, while being educated on how to die poor. This thinking guarantees a life of mediocrity and has consumed the majority. It takes a massive mental shift, or in more simpler terms, wisdom and awareness, to think and believe big. You must believe no matter what others believe and you must pursue regardless if others pursue or not. Millies and billies didn't get to where they are by thinking like everyone else, so don't expect to get in their circles if you do. A mental shift is required to live the ultimate life and to be equally respected in the circle of the wealthiest people in the world. Study their lives, mindsets, thinking processes and their journeys to success to help you prepare for the mandatory change of thinking you must adopt. Forget about being congratulated or understood by those around you. Most of them aren't interested in anything that adds more work to their basic life, not even just one thought. And don't get trapped by not expanding your mind, there will be no one to blame but yourself. I asked God to give me a massive mental shift so that I could perceive wider, see clearer, hear higher, and live bigger, and have since received and adopted the belief that everything is possible. All that I believe, have believed and thought, is exactly what I am living and becoming today.

THE NECESSITY OF CURIOSITY
Curiosity is a strong desire to know or learn something. It is a secret weapon of millies and billies. Curious as to what hasn't been done, what should be done, what needs to be changed, how something can be done

better, how something can be done bigger, how great they can be, how greater they can become. Your level of curiosity plays a major role in the level of success and opportunities created and sent in your life. Remaining open, teachable and available are traits of the world's most wealthiest and influential. As of today, decide that you will not limit your life to only what you think you know, only to who you think you are and only to what you think you are capable of doing. Life is a journey of discovery. The more curious you are, the more you'll learn and experience along the way. Every creation, idea, project, business, product and service you come across was sparked from someone's curiosity, which means curiosity turns ordinary people into millionaires and billionaires. While others are set in their ways, thoughts, perceptions, limits and decisions, make it your religion to cherish and utilize curiosity to open up your life to the unlimited.

DEFINE, CRAFT & MASTER OTHER'S PERCEPTION OF YOU

Perception is the ability to see, hear, or become aware of something through the senses. What do you want people to sense about you? What are the key things you'd like to come to their mind when your name is mentioned. What feeling do you want them to have when you enter the room? How do you want them to respond when they find out you're involved in the same project, event or venture that they are as well? Though people will form their own opinions of you throughout life, whether they know you personally or not, you still have the advantage and opportunity to define, craft and master other's perception of you. The perception you create for them serves as a guide in pointing things out that you want them to know and think. As for networking with millies and billies, you want to produce a perception that says you are successful and willing to help others succeed, that you're a hard and smart worker, a teacher, a student, kind, a leader, a motivator, have integrity, honest, caring, a visionary and all the great things that you truly are. Your perception should also assist in letting others know what to expect from you, what you expect from them, the type of people you prefer to be around and anything that gives them beneficial and persuasive information to want to network and build a relationship with you. It is imperative that you give attention to the projected perception you present in order to maximize your networking potential with millies, billies and everyone else on a worldwide basis.

DEFINE

A good way to define your perception, that is, how you want to be perceived by others, is to start from the end and work towards the beginning, similar to how several films are made. By deciding on what you want the finished product to be, or better yet, your legacy, gives you a starting point to fill in the blanks, answer all questions, change directions if needed and implement strategic action on a daily basis. By thinking from your intended legacy, you'll discover the proper ways to carry yourself, communicate, learn disciplines and develop the right characteristics to help propel you to your goals and recognize the type of people you need to connect with along the way. Your definition should include what you want in life overall, who you intend to become, and what you want the world to think about you here now and after. Write it down, save it in an email, and return to it for motivation and direction to help you move on to the next scene in life when it's time.

CRAFT

Crafting your perception is the process of taking your definition and then creating step by step procedures and action to get the results you desire. If you want your perception to include you being a leader in a particular industry, then taking the necessary steps to learn everything you can in that industry, creating or producing something in that industry, networking in that industry, and writing books related to that industry is a great way to craft that industry leader perception. It's always good to analyze the perceptions you have of other people as well and then utilize why you have that perception of them to help you craft your own for others. Be open to use everything imaginable, every resource and every person you can to craft your perception. Whether it's writing a book, making appearances, the schools you attend, joining organizations, starting a business, your friends and connections, moving to strategic cities, wearing convincing clothes, learning different languages, advocating for certain topics, or even the photos and videos you share on social media, your perception is crucial when networking with millies and billies. Craft it precisely as if your life depends on it.

MASTER

Once you have perfected the defining and crafting of the perception you desire, you must take massive action to master it and have it rooted into the minds of everyone you come across. This is done by duplicating what you do best over and over, pushing it to the maximum limit while expanding on it as well. Also take advantage of others that can lend credibility to your perception by associating with them, appearing with them and cross marketing yourself with people who already have the same perception you desire to have. The world automatically gets impressions, assumptions and conclusions about you from the type of people you hang around the most, so make it interesting. You can easily build instant perception by your associations alone, though at the end of the day you want more to stand on other than the shoulders of successful friends. Brick by brick, you are building an image, creating a perception that people attach and align with you, resulting in the formation of your personal brand. Millionaires, billionaires and the world are intrigued by people who know who they are and who are masters at telling everyone else.

BE SEEN AND BE HEARD

Like or not, people who make the most noise are the ones that get the most attention. It's almost impossible for you to network with millies and even harder with billies, if no one knows who you are, and that's just the honest truth. Without prior connections, it will take strategic visibility, creating something significant that garners attention, knowing someone already or a referral to get in the world's power circles. It's always been that way. Thankfully, technology has created a more open playing field to get you in the game by playing by the rules of networking. Millies and billies participate in social interaction as well, and more of them than you know take advantage of certain social media platforms to network and build new relationships. By calculated use of the internet and social media, with your crafted perception and the rules of this book, not only can you get their attention, you can also become an asset in their life.

MARKET YOURSELF ONLINE WHERE THEY PLAY

The easiest, fastest and least expensive way to meet millies and billies is online. As of this writing, Linkedin.com has been my greatest resource for connecting and befriending them. They are all over that platform, in every country. While there are other sites and new ones emerging every year, Linkedin is the current leader that I suggest you take advantage of. Your primary bait on Linkedin will be the perception of your main profile, next to that will be what you share with the world through your posts and lastly, your interaction with others. Your Linkedin profile headline that displays your career title is a gold mine and should be simplistic yet commanding and powerful, using words that suggest that you're a leader. Instead of using words like "Freelance Graphic Designer", just say "Graphic Designer". Instead of using words like "Independent Business Owner", just say "Entrepreneur" or "Business Owner". Instead of saying "Aspiring Actor", just say "Actor". Omit words that minimize or marginalize your position. In the eyes of millies and billies, the more assured you are of who and what you are, the better. Any uncertainty of yourself in the business world could potentially be detrimental and close doors before they open.

Your Linkedin profile description or any professional social network description should describe your best attributes and what you've done. Mention things you're working on and what you are contributing or intend to contribute to the world. Including what you believe your ultimate purpose in life is can also pay off big. Those of like purpose will connect with you faster and may offer support instantly. Sharing important projects or opportunities that you've collaborated on with other individuals, groups or people around the world is also a plus. Be authentic in your description and let the words you use come from your heart, just don't overdo it by writing an essay. I recommend ten sentences or less in your description if possible, so it can be read quickly. I've found this attracts the world's most successful and wealthy individuals. I use this same format when assisting others with their Linkedin profile descriptions. If millies and billies don't already know who you are, they make the decision to connect with you by what they read or don't read. All of the content on your Linkedin page should be used to convey your crafted perception. As long as you're dressed decent, most could care less about what you physically look like. I also noticed that they don't care where you went to school either. I've never included my school education on Linkedin. Millies and billies top concern is that you're a leader and that you're successful at it.

MEDIA OUTLETS ADD VISIBILITY AND CREDIBILITY TO PERCEPTION

If you are not already in the midst of millies and billies, your greatest chance of getting their attention and networking with them will most likely be online. Of course there's the possibility of meeting them in person at events if you're able to attend and can afford any related expenses but it's much less expensive to achieve this online. Online video is the new television, and in my opinion, more powerful than television. You can reach hundreds of millions or even a billion people within hours from the comfort of your home in this new age of technology, costing little to nothing, and producing massive visibility for whatever it is you are sharing. Creating and posting valuable, motivational, interesting or even controversial video content on Linkedin and your social media platforms is the greatest strategy for getting the attention of millies and billies. Just keep your perception intact, and your posting strategic to your goal.

I often share uplifting and motivational vlogs to encourage my network of friends and global followers. If you have something positive to share that can motivate someone else, I suggest you do so. Positivity is a magnet in itself and can open doors faster than your hands ever could. Over recent years, thousands of unknown individuals globally have used online video to become famous, influential and wealthy, creating major social media platforms, networking and connecting with some of the biggest brands, celebrities, corporations and media networks. What does this mean? It means that the millies and billies that own these brands, corporations and media networks are watching, so are the celebrities. If you're afraid of being on camera then you'll just have to do it afraid. I've always been shy but I made a decision that I was going to do whatever it took to surround myself with the right people and escape a life of mediocrity, and so I went for it. It is in your best interest to do the same if you believe this will further advance you.

You may think to yourself that creating video content isn't for everyone but I beg to differ. Spend a day surfing Youtube and you'll learn that anyone can do it. Once people know you're out there, anything can happen, and I do mean anything, you just have to start. You can also gain additional visibility and credibility from other people and sources like media outlets, blogs, news stories, someone interviewing you, etc. Allowing others to present you, write about you, feature you, interview you, recognize you and award you makes you appear important, credible and valuable in the eyes of the world, and in the eyes of millies and billies. This strategy is used constantly by celebrities, public figures, even millies and billies, whether there's real merit behind it or not, people do it because it works. You'd be surprised how many things are staged and planned, just for perception and credibility, and nothing else. Use any and all reputable media resources possible and platforms, or help someone create one just to endorse you and present you for more credibility. Post the interview, press release, write up, video, photos and whatever you have on Linkedin and your social media to further build up your perception and to attract exactly what and who you desire. Do this over and over and over. People are always looking for others to follow, and millies and billies are looking for the leader that people are following.

WAYS TO QUICKLY MAGNIFY YOUR VISIBILITY AND PERCEPTION

1. **BOOKS.** Writing and publishing a book still sets you apart. Promote the book in every way possible and use it to garner speaking engagements, media appearances, inclusion on panels for events or collaborations with other authors and leaders.

2. **CROSS MARKETING.** Collaborate with other people, businesses, brands and so on to present yourself in front of new audiences, new customers/clients and new connections.

3. **EVENTS.** Attend all kinds of events (conferences, seminars, networking, launches, ribbon cuttings, award shows, grand openings, etc), if only to meet the organizers, which are normally the most connected people in the room.

Face to face meetings are still extremely valuable and they build trust much faster. Get photos and videos whenever possible and appropriate, and share them on Linkedin and your social media for more persuasive power to fuel your credibility and crafted perception.

4. **PUBLICITY.** If you're an expert in something, have a product, service, discovery or just highly opinionated, reach out to radio, magazines, newspapers and all forms of media to share your story or to chime in on one.

5. **SOCIAL MEDIA.** Use social media sites to build your name, mission, cause, visibility and personal brand. Show and tell the world who you are, what you're about, what you bring to the table and what you want. Someone will respond.

6. **VIDEO.** Use video as often as possible to share things to magnify your perception and the value you bring to others. Do it all strategically to convince people to support, follow and promote you to others. Use video testimonials from others as well to endorse the perception you desire.

7. **VOLUNTEER & JOIN.** Volunteer to help companies, charities, organizations, groups and people to get your name and face out there, get your foot in the door, and to do good. You never know who else could be involved, who's watching or who you will meet.

BE A PEER, NOT A FOLLOWER

Leadership will always distinguish you. It took me a while to realize that I was attracting millies and billies around the world because of it. Through my events, books, philanthropic efforts, motivational quotes and videos, and mutual associations with people they're familiar with, I was already presenting myself as a peer to them. I'll be honest and admit it, this wasn't intentional, however, I'd already decided prior as to who I wanted to become. Carrying myself, thinking, producing and operating like those I desired to be like and be around, is what attracted them to me. Millies and billies are drawn to people who are on the move, leaders, doers, gamechangers, thinkers, especially those that are doing things on a larger scale. There's only so much time in each day, and most aren't going to waste their time on anything that doesn't fuel and add to who they already are. I'm not saying you have to fake it until you make it, what I am saying is that you must think of yourself in the same light you think of them, as a peer, while learning, making strategic decisions and taking daily action to get to the results and destinations you desire. People of the same mindset, who operate in that same atmosphere, and respond to that atmosphere, ultimately attract one another. It doesn't matter if your bank accounts look alike at the time or not.

KEY POINTS ✓

- Millies and billies are known to surround themselves with the smartest, greatest, most talented, most curious, most advanced and most unlimited people.
- Most people are raised to follow the rules, instructions, and the scheduling of other people for the rest of their lives, while being educated on how to die poor.
- Your level of curiosity plays a major role in the level of success and opportunities created and sent into your life.

- Millionaires, billionaires and the world are intrigued by people who know who they are and who are masters at telling everyone else.
- People of the same mindset, who operate in that same atmosphere, and respond to that atmosphere, ultimately attract one another. It doesn't matter if your bank accounts look alike at the time or not.

3

Communicate Higher And Live With A Purpose Greater Than Money

One of the most important things you'll need to not only network with millies and billies but also to help you bypass the crowds in life, are great communication skills. I often watch interviews of public figures and business leaders to study and observe their communication style, techniques, characteristics, as well as their choice of words and body language. What I notice the most is their optimism and ability to turn what could have been a sour topic or low moment into something sweeter, taking the high road and staying positive. The world will throw negativity your way daily and pound you into the ground if you let it. The only way to survive this in today's society is to start communicating higher in all situations, beginning first from the inside. I recently began speaking affirmations over my life in the morning to clean out all the mental trash accumulated the previous day and from overnight in my dreams. This has helped me focus on being my greatest self no matter what I'm facing on a daily basis. It has also helped me bring a breath of fresh air to my communication with everyone, including millies and billies, which they often take notice of and commend me on right away.

There's just something special about a person that decides to communicate higher. Low living and low thinking people will consider you crazy and weird, but those who know what it takes to operate in that atmosphere, who understand its importance, will consider you inspirational. Communicating higher through my social media posts, videos, books, my business ventures and philanthropic efforts, as well as my direct communication when networking, has attracted an unlimited amount of millies and billies into my life. I suggest you practice what I'll call being 'Positively Possible', that is, having elevated thinking, listening, speaking and understanding in all things. Looking for the possibilities and the greater good in all of your communication with others, as well as in your life. It shows that your heart and your spirit are in a higher place. A place that desires to bring more light to the world, which is needed now more than ever.

THE POWER OF WORDS

Words are one of the three most powerful forces in the world, God and love being the other two. Words are also the first law (Master Words) in my book "The 40 Laws of Networking: Keys to creating global Influence,

Wealth and Power". Words serve as a primary secret weapon to networking. They are the force that initiates most of day to day activity and they carry the power of life and death. There is no escaping words, no denying their influence or necessity. Though most people never reach the awareness of the importance of words, you must take heed immediately and accept that words are your friends and they alone can propel you into circles of millies and billies. Use convincing, energetic, relatable, persuasive, exciting, motivating and inspiring words in your communications to steer, guide and empower conversations, never leaving the conversations to their own demise. People will judge you, make assumptions, draw conclusions, present opportunities, close doors, recommend you, love you, hate you, admire you, and some will even try to kill you from the choice of words you use. This could further explain the Bible scripture "Death and life are in the power of the tongue: and they that love it shall eat the fruit thereof" (Proverbs 18:21, KJV).

From my self-analysis, a great majority of my networking success is from me becoming a master of words. The most successful leaders in the world are masters of words. Indeed, timing continues to play a huge contribution in my success as well but using the best words during all times, good and bad, grants me favor with others, thus allowing me to help to determine my own timing for success. By taking more time to think about your replies when sending emails, having conversations on the phone or in person, whether it's personal or business, you will be able to use words to get exactly what you want and have others on board to help you get it. Words work together to activate a response from the reader or listener. The more aware you become of the power of words, the more you must calculate each word when networking. If you become a master of words, you will become a master of people.

POSITIVELY POSSIBLE

Whether you'd like to admit it or not, the world has taken a dramatic shift since late 2016. It's no secret, if you're paying attention, that something has changed in the atmosphere. The level of drama, chaos, hatred, violence, fear, lies, deception and darkness has increased. In addition, those who seek to bring light, love, happiness, peace and healing are sprouting up all over the place as well, especially on social media. Positivity is almost like a new religion that the masses are adopting to counter the negativity perpetuated daily across the media. Even the phrase "Positive Vibes" has become a movement. Having faith and belief in yourself, and in a higher power, is spreading faster than ever. And motivation, well you can browse just about any social network on any given day and at any time, and find a video of someone sharing motivation to help you get out of the slump you're in. This force of positivity, vibrating higher and communicating higher is what you will need to stand out from the crowd and be noticed by the millies and billies who make it mandatory to surround themselves with the same type of people.

Yes, there are millies and billies that are negative, those who love chaos, prejudice, fear, hatred, and others who are just plain evil but I believe the majority are the total opposite. Regardless of what you hear about wealthy or rich people, not all are the same. Most negative comments thrown at them almost always come from those who have no wealthy family or friends in their life. As the years roll on and the atmosphere intensifies, and it will for certain, you'll have to operate at a higher frequency as well or you too will soon fall into the clutches of mediocrity, depression, and fear. Millies and billies I know are genuine, caring people, full of peace and light, and they give more back to the world than people could fathom. They are fully aware of the world's problems and the problem makers. By you being full of positivity, faith and motivation, you become more like them and they'll recognize it from afar. Many often contact me because of it and then tell me how much I've inspired them. Let it overflow into everything you do, in your conversations, in your marketing, in your social media, meeting new people, with your team, crew, staff, employees, co-workers, even with random people because you never know who knows who.

THE VISIONARY LIFE

Have you ever wondered why there are so few millionaires and even fewer billionaires in the world? Several have shared their feedback and opinions to answer that question for decades. I believe a great majority of the answers can be summed into one word, and that word is "visionary". Most if not all significant leaders in history, and in the present world today, are those who operate from the visionary life. Those who are in tune with what's going on inside of them, those who listen to ideas and instructions via their instinct or divine nature, these tend to know things that others don't know, hear things that others don't hear, see things that others don't see, which enables them to do things that others don't do, and ultimately achieve things that very few achieve. They are known as visionaries, and several millies and billies worldwide fall into this category without a doubt. Many, even from their childhood, have believed they were cut from a different cloth. They've been encountering higher communication from within all of their lives and eventually made a decision to respond to what they were hearing.

We all have access to this ongoing communication, instinct or intuition but only a handful actually listen, pay attention, and hit reply. Global movements have been launched, wars have been won, empires have been built, diseases have been cured and great inventions have been invented by accessing this visionary atmosphere. You too can access it by opening yourself to observation, curiosity, ongoing personal development and a determination to be used for your life's maximum purpose. Leaders are visionaries, matter of fact, vision often opens the door for leadership to come in. And if becoming a leader is the first rule written for networking with millies and billies, then being a visionary is the author. You are a visionary but life itself can disrupt the reception signals and halt communication if you don't tune in often to keep it clear. Millies and billies know the importance of vision and tuning in. The more you tune in and reply, the more you will attract others who do the same.

THE BIG PICTURE

At the end of the day, money alone won't fulfill your soul. Millies and billies know that having a deeper passion and purpose, a big picture in life, is what ultimately gives them a reason to continue. Whether it's helping loved ones, saving the animals, restoring the land, eradicating starvation, exploring space for the next generation, finding cures for diseases, ending homelessness or something else, discover what truly moves your inner man and gives oxygen to your heart. Being able to share a purpose greater than money humanizes you and builds respect among the wealthy. Though a few people may not agree with me, most wealthy people believe that their wealth is not just for them. If you think hard and long enough, you probably received an inclination of your purpose as a child or teenager. What was it that you wanted to change about the world or make better. What made you sad or what was it that you hated the most when it was done to someone else? Answering these questions will help guide you to your big picture in life, to the purpose that is greater than you and far more meaningful than any amount of money you can make.

Knowing your big picture is critical to developing and sustaining long lasting, respectful and equally inspirational relationships with millies and billies. Having lots of money, yet living with a purpose greater than money puts you in a special class. When you know why you were created, and begin to move toward it, that purpose begins to flow towards you as well with all the things needed to bring it to pass. Seek to discover what your big picture is all about as soon as possible. It'll be easier and faster to make every life decision and networking decision along your journey.

KEY POINTS ✓

- Words serve as a primary secret weapon to networking. They are the force that initiates most of day to day activity and they carry the power of life and death.
- If you become a master of words, you will become a master of people.
- Positivity is almost like a new religion that the masses are adopting to counter the negativity perpetuated daily across the media.
- Knowing your big picture is critical to developing and sustaining long lasting, respectful and equally inspirational relationships with millies and billies.

4

Work Your Sphere Of Influence To Perpetually Expand Your Circle And Globality

One way to expedite networking with millies and billies is by using your current sphere of influence to connect with those who know who you know or in other words, using a middleman or mutual connection between you and another as your networking strategy. For some privileged circles, you can only get in by knowing someone already in it, which means your money won't help you. Millies and billies repeatedly use their sphere of influence, leveraging everyone in it, to get what they want and accomplish what they've set out to do. If you don't know anyone that knows a millie or billie then you'll need to make more friends, show up at an event, do some travel or devise an online strategy to find someone that knows the person you want to connect with, and then proceed to network with that person. I never said this would be easy. Networking and building relationships is work, and undoubtedly some of the most valuable and beneficial work that you will ever do. Once in the desired circles you'll notice a pattern of connections. Though it's true that millies and billies may have a large variety and diverse group of people within their sphere of influence, there's still a common thread of people they prefer in their immediate circle. Your goal is to get in where you fit in, preferably with like-minded and like-spirited people, where you are respected and can also add value and inspiration. Never underestimate the power of networking and more importantly, starting with your sphere of influence. Most of us don't even know who we're already linked to. All it takes is one person to set off a series of events and encounters that change everything.

ACCESS BY ORGANIZATION

If you discover that no one in your life or in your sphere of influence is connected to a millie or billie, and you have nowhere else to turn, your next strategy is to go where the millies and billies are. Without stalking them of course, find out what they're involved in so you can get involved as well. Our sphere of influence expands incredibly by effectively using groups and organizations that we're already associated with or can become a part of. Some examples include high school or college alumni groups, being a board member of an organization or company, fraternities and sororities, country club membership, charities and philanthropy involvement, panel member for events, religious institutions, additional investor in a business, neighborhood organizations, and so on. Anything of the sort that you share mutually should be used to show commonality and as a conversation piece when networking. I've met an immeasurable amount of millies and billies through my philanthropic interests and efforts, having the same religious beliefs, being a member of the same organizations as they are and more. It works because we all desire to surround ourselves with those of the same interests. Do whatever needs to be done and take the proper steps to get access.

SUPPORT THEM PRIVATELY AND PUBLICLY WHEN POSSIBLE

Everyone loves and cherishes support from others, even more so from our peers and those we admire, so do millies and billies. Understanding the importance of support, they equally appreciate those who help them push their mission, their voice, their projects and their purpose forward. Though they may have more than enough funding to get things in motion, still, some things rely solely on the power of supportive people to make it stick, appear believable and to really make it successful. This means your support can have immeasurable value, especially in this age of social media and where anyone can obtain global visibility at the touch of a button. Simple gestures as a social media

Retweet, Share, or a favorable Comment can go a long way and be remembered, and could potentially start a new friendship. You never know who's watching, you really don't. Use social media religiously to your advantage for networking with millies and billies, it alone can seal the deal if you follow the rules. They're all over the internet and active, especially on Linkedin, which I've found that platform to be the most resourceful one for interaction and direct communication with them.

Volunteering for their non-profit or benefit fundraiser, recommending sponsors, offering media coverage, sponsoring food and/or beverages, donating time or money, or helping in any way also puts you in a better position to build a professional relationship with them, plus in the midst of potential future opportunities. Don't count out any methods of support, all of them matter. I've had hundreds of people worldwide offer to volunteer at my events, just to network with me and be in the midst of doing bigger and greater things. I'm now friends with them all, even business partners with some. People are more accessible than ever before, so make yourself visible and known by supporting those you want to connect with. This networking strategy can often take you much further than what you originally had in mind.

USE GLOBALITY AS LEVERAGE

Technology has placed the entire world in the palm of our hands, literally. There's no excuse anymore for not having friends, colleagues, business partners, opportunities, followers, fans, supporters, haters, and for some even lovers around the world. It has never been easier to be global. And being global is powerful in the eyes of millies and billies. When communicating and they ask about what you're currently working on or have going on, don't forget to mention any projects, events or present business affiliations in other countries and different parts of the world. Millies and billies tend to be well traveled and have business dealings, colleagues and friends globally, therefore they easily gravitate to those who have the same and can relate. It makes conversations a lot more intriguing and comfortable, plus they may even recommend places for lodging, dining or even suggest meeting a friend of theirs on your future travels to specific regions, which can further expand your sphere of influence.

Globality is the condition of being global. Since becoming global with my personal brand, books and events, I believe it has played a pivotal role in the type, level and amount of people and opportunities I attract. It has made my life unlimited. You should make it mandatory to network with leaders and creators outside of your country. Taking things even further, you should also present opportunities to collaborate, partner or support one another as well. Having a global network of contacts will attract more of the same, and then it becomes endless. I constantly receive invitations to connect with leaders, millionaires, billionaires and everything in-between from every part of the world on a continual basis. People want to attach themselves to those who are exceptionally connected. Use the commonality of globality as much as you can. Take advantage of international travel when possible to create global opportunities and friendships, and also produce any noteworthy worldwide recognition for massive networking leverage.

KEY POINTS ✓

- Millies and billies repeatedly use their sphere of influence, leveraging everyone in it, to get what they want and accomplish what they've set out to do.
- All it takes is one person to set off a series of events and encounters that change everything.

- Simple gestures as a social media Retweet, Share, or a favorable Comment can go a long way and be remembered, and could potentially start a new friendship.
- People are more accessible than ever before, so make yourself visible and known by supporting those you want to connect with.
- You should make it mandatory to network with leaders and creators outside of your country.
- Take advantage of international travel when possible to create global opportunities and friendships, and also produce any noteworthy worldwide recognition for massive networking leverage.

5

.

RULE 5

REQUEST MENTORSHIP

Once established with the previous four rules, and now seen more as a peer, colleague or even someone they admire, switch things up and ask them to be one of your mentors. Not only are people flattered to be asked that, if done correctly to where they know it won't take up too much of their time, you'll end up with a millie or billie for a mentor, friend and maybe even a business partner in due time. What is a mentor exactly? A mentor is someone you trust and consider experienced enough to give you advice and guidance. If I would have known the value of a mentor as a child, I would have asked my parents to help me find one for every area of life that they themselves were not already advanced in because mentors are priceless. I didn't have the luxury of having a mentor around me or anyone with a proven track record that I could call on for career success or great life advice. Luckily, you don't have to have one either if you can't find one. Instead, do what I did and use books and videos of successful and inspiring people to mentor you. Don't sit there and complain about where you live and your lack of access. As long as there's the internet or a library with internet, you have access to an unlimited amount of mentors worldwide. As for your new found millie and billie connections, once you've made your way into their circles, several will be happy to mentor you because many love the feeling of respect and admiration that comes from the opportunity and ability to inspire greatness in others. Present yourself properly and ask the right way. I suggest establishing the previous four rules first and then using something similar to this sample mentorship request email below:

SAMPLE MENTORSHIP EMAIL REQUEST

Greetings Mr. or Mrs. (their last name),

My name is (your first and last name). I'm not only motivated by you but also inspired by your work and trailblazing journey as an entrepreneur, author and investor (use their titles or what you believe may be most important to them). I would be extremely honored if you could spare just a few moments of your time to mentor me by imparting sound career and life advice at your leisure. Upon your scheduling and availability, it can easily be done via email, a brief call or a text message periodically, sharing your expertise, wisdom and valuable insight in response to a few questions I may have. I'd be forever grateful for this opportunity to learn and grow. Thank you for your time and I look forward to hearing from you. Have an amazing day!

Sincerely,
(Your first and last name)

REQUEST ADVICE IF YOUR MENTORSHIP REQUEST IS DENIED

Not everyone has the available time to mentor you, so don't get offended or assume they denied you for any other reason. Some are already mentoring several individuals, small groups or even large organizations. If you find yourself being denied or not getting a reply at all, go a different route and just ask for advice on a particular matter, industry or whatever it is you initially wanted mentorship for in the first place. A lot of times the simpler the request, the greater the chances are for a response. Keep in mind that some of these people are just as busy, if not more, than you are. They are continually pulled in multiple directions, dodging beggars and time wasters constantly, and can't possibly respond to everyone all the time. Be precise in your approach, state your purpose and never beat around the bush. They should be able to understand exactly what you need from your first message and determine if they are able and available to assist you. Always make clarity your priority. Even if they can't mentor you on an ongoing basis, you could request recommendations for books, videos, magazines, organizations, blogs or people that could help guide you. Just remember to do the most important thing, which is to always ask.

INCLUDE THEM IN YOUR BIG LIFE MOMENTS

Once the door is open for communication and you've secured them as a mentor, the rest is up to you to turn them into a great friend. Everyone loves to be included in big moments, events and projects, so make it a priority to invite your mentors to such events in your life. Now don't go sending them invites every week or every month, be wise about their time and never become an annoyance. They are most likely already bombarded with invitations, fundraisers, galas, meetings and more. Choose the invitations you send wisely and by all means, make them VIP guests as well. I suggest you don't charge them to attend a paid event. If they want to pay, they'll suggest it. If you can comp their tickets or pay for their tickets yourself, your efforts will be remembered. Also, the further out the moment or event is on the calendar, the better. When I receive invitations to events coming up within a few days or a week away, I normally delete it. Anyone that cares enough about your attendance is not going to send you an invite to an event that takes place in the next two days. Mind you, some things happen at the spur of the moment and you have to roll with the punches but try to keep those invites to yourself. It can often appear disrespectful and insensitive to send a last minute invite to certain types of people. Events such as grand openings and ribbon cuttings, major award recognitions, weddings, book or product launches, big company anniversaries and anything that you believe may also resonate with your mentor are good invites to send. Including them shows that you care about them, respect them, considers them a friend, and lets them know they are an important part of your life.

MILLIONAIRES & BILLIONAIRES BY LOCATION

Millies and billies live all over the world however, large numbers of them reside in the same areas. For online networking, it's faster to seek them out directly by their name if you know it or seek them out in cities where most live. I suggest doing both. You can also research industries you're interested in and major companies to find obvious ones as well. Below is a list of some of the top cities and regions where the wealthiest people in the world live. Strategically connecting and befriending leaders and professionals in these cities will get you closer to or immediately in their circles before you can blink twice. Here's to you connecting to millies and billies, to becoming one as well and using your life and platform to help positively impact and change the world. Now go get to networking. Good luck friends.

MOST MILLIONAIRES BY LOCATION
Courtesy of WorldAtlas.com

London, UK: 357,200 millionaires.

New York, USA: 339,200 millionaires.

Tokyo, Japan: 279,800 millionaires.

Hong Kong: 227,900 millionaires.

Singapore: 217,300 millionaires.

San Francisco, USA: 180,300 millionaires.

Los Angeles, USA: 173,300 millionaires.

Frankfurt, Germany: 128,300 millionaires.

Osaka, Japan: 117,700 millionaires.

Paris, France: 110,900 millionaires.

MOST BILLIONAIRES BY LOCATION

Courtesy of BusinessInsider.com

New York, USA: 105 billionaires
Hong Kong: 87 billionaires
San Francisco, USA: 75 billionaires
Moscow, Russia: 70 billionaires
London, UK: 65 billionaires
Beijgin, China: 55 billionaires
Singapore: 39 billionaires
Los Angeles, USA: 39 billionaires
Dubai, UAE: 38 billionaires
Mumbai, India: 38 billionaires

KEY POINTS ✓

- Even if they can't mentor you on an ongoing basis, you could request recommendations for books, videos, magazines, organizations, blogs or people that could help guide you.
- Always make clarity your priority.
- Events such as grand openings and ribbon cuttings, major award recognitions, wedding, book or product launches, big company anniversaries and anything that you believe may

also resonate with your mentor are good invites to send.

- For online networking, it's faster to seek them out directly by their name if you know it or seek them out in cities where most live.

become endless

INTERNATIONAL

Made in the USA
Columbia, SC
01 June 2021

38562661R00048